PICTURE LIBRARY

PANDAS

PICTURE LIBRARY
PANDAS

Norman Barrett

Franklin Watts

London   New York   Sydney   Toronto

© 1988 Franklin Watts Ltd

First published in Great Britain
   1988 by
Franklin Watts Ltd
12a Golden Square
London W1R 4BA

First published in the USA by
Franklin Watts Inc
387 Park Avenue South
New York
NY 10016

First published in Australia by
Franklin Watts
14 Mars Road
Lane Cove
NSW 2066

UK ISBN: 0 86313 642 7
US ISBN: 0-531-10530-X
Library of Congress Catalog Card
Number 87–50850

Printed in Italy

Designed by
Barrett & Willard

Photographs by
National Zoological Park, Washington, DC
Pat Morris
Frank Spooner Pictures/Gamma
Bruce Coleman/World Wildlife Fund
Rex Features

Illustrations by
Rhoda & Robert Burns

Technical Consultant
Michael Chinery

Acknowledgements
Special thanks are due to the
Smithsonian Institution, Washington, DC,
for information and pictures of
Ling-Ling and Hsing-Hsing

Contents

Introduction

There are two kinds of pandas, the giant panda and the red, or lesser, panda. The giant panda is one of the rarest animals in the world. In the wild, it lives only in the mountains of central China.

Giant pandas were once thought to be types of raccoons. But scientists now believe that they are more closely related to bears.

△ The giant panda is a distinctive animal. It has a white coat, with black legs and shoulders. Its round, chubby face has black markings.

Giant pandas are always a popular attraction in zoos. They have a funny, lovable appearance, and their playful antics are guaranteed to entertain visitors of all ages.

A full-grown panda is somewhat smaller than an American black bear. With its white face and black patches around its eyes, it is the easiest of animals to recognize.

△ The two giant pandas in the Washington, D.C., Zoo. Few zoos outside China are lucky enough to have pandas.

Looking at pandas

The map on the right shows the area (bounded by the dotted line) where giant pandas used to live thousands of years ago. They ranged through most of what is now southern China and even into Burma. Gradually, however, people have cut down their natural habitat of bamboo forests. Now only a few hundred pandas are left in the wild. They live in the Sichuan province, mostly in areas set aside by the Chinese government to protect the habitats of these rare animals. These special reserves are shown in orange.

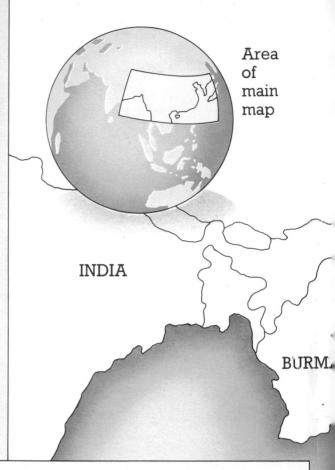

Area of main map

INDIA

BURM.

Pandas big and small

Human being

Giant panda

Lesser panda

A male adult giant panda is about 1.5 m (5 ft) long, and stands 60 cm (2 ft) high at the shoulders. It weighs as much as 135 kg (300 lb). The lesser panda is about 60 cm (2 ft) long, has a tail of 45 cm (1½ ft), stands over 30 cm (1 ft) and weighs only about 5 kg (11 lb).

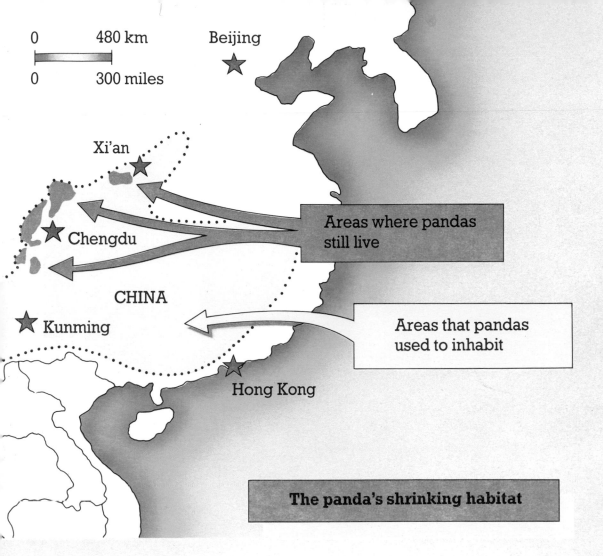

0   480 km

0   300 miles

Beijing ★

Xi'an ★

Chengdu ★

CHINA

Kunming ★

Hong Kong ★

Areas where pandas still live

Areas that pandas used to inhabit

The panda's shrinking habitat

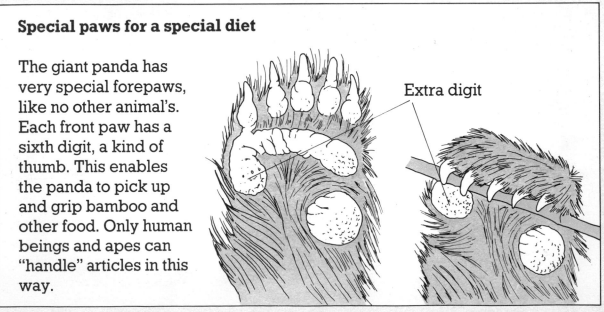

Special paws for a special diet

The giant panda has very special forepaws, like no other animal's. Each front paw has a sixth digit, a kind of thumb. This enables the panda to pick up and grip bamboo and other food. Only human beings and apes can "handle" articles in this way.

Extra digit

9

Everyday life

Pandas live in dense forests of bamboo and conifer trees, high in the mountains. It is usually wet and cold, but their thick fur helps to keep them warm.

They spend most of the day ambling slowly along the ground, eating bamboo shoots and leaves, or just sleeping. They live by themselves for most of the time, but males and females come together during the short mating season.

△ A giant panda roams through its natural habitat in the bamboo forest. Snow is on the ground for about half of the year.

▷ A Chinese drawing shows a mother with two cubs. The land and climate make human travel in the region extremely difficult.

▷ A panda stops for a meal on a pleasant sunny day. The thick bamboo makes it hard for people to move around. Following panda tracks is often the only way people can travel through the forest.

Growing up

A female panda usually gives birth to a single cub or twins. A newborn cub is tiny, and weighs only about 120 g (4 oz). But it soon grows, and after 10 weeks weighs about 3.5 kg (8 lb).

For the first few weeks, the cub is helpless. The mother protects it, cradling it in her arms and feeding it with her milk. A cub stays with its mother for about 18 months, learning all it needs to survive in the wild.

▽ A mother is tempted by an apple on a stick as she carefully nurses her 20-day-old cub at Chengdu Zoo, in China. The mother is called Mei-Mei, and the cub, her sixth, Du-Du.

▷ Baby pandas in captivity do not have to depend on their mothers for as long as those in the wild. This one, called Bing-Bing, is two months old.

▽ Xi-Xi is 6 months old and has learned to take milk from a bottle.

Time to eat

In the wild, pandas feed almost entirely on bamboo. They have to chew on bamboo shoots for 12 or more hours a day to get enough nourishment from this food.

Pandas also eat grasses, flowers and insects and other small animals. In captivity, in addition to bamboo, they are fed on apples, carrots, rice gruel, and perhaps some ground meat.

▽ Pandas usually sit down to eat, with their hind legs stretched out in front of them. They grasp the bamboo firmly, using their powerful teeth to tear off and eat the leaves and twigs and peel the tough stalks.

Time to play

In captivity, pandas are very playful, even when they are no longer cubs. They enjoy climbing and rolling and playing with various objects and on apparatus.

With their clownish behavior and comical appearance, they are the most loved animals in zoos all over the world.

△ "Are you coming out to play?" Ling-Ling and Hsing-Hsing enjoy each other's company in the Smithsonian Institution's Zoo, in Washington, D.C. They were gifts from China to the people of the United States in 1972.

Pandas enjoy playing in the snow, and sometimes their keepers make snowmen for them to play with. Zoo pandas like to play outdoors during the winter months, when the temperature is like that of their natural habitat.

Time to sleep

When they are not eating or playing, pandas usually sleep. In the wild, pandas are most active at dawn and at dusk. They use up much energy eating, so they sleep often.

Pandas do not have a permanent home. They wander around the bamboo forest. They sleep in all kinds of places, usually with something to lean against.

In most zoos, pandas have their own den. They sleep on a platform, or bed, raised just off the floor.

▽ A panda snoozing outdoors in the zoo. Like people, pandas sleep in different positions – on their backs, their fronts, their sides, and even sitting down.

Saving the panda

For some time now, scientists have been worried about the declining numbers of giant pandas in the wild. Every effort is being made to save this much loved animal from extinction, or dying out.

The chief problem is that the panda's natural habitat, the mountainous bamboo forests of central China, is shrinking. The spread of farms has driven the animals into smaller areas.

△ Pandas are difficult to breed outside China. Even though Ling-Ling and Hsing-Hsing have given birth to four babies in many years in Washington Zoo, none of them survived longer than three days.

▷ Transporting a giant panda in the high mountain forests of central China can only be done on foot.

Sometimes, sick animals are taken back to a research station to be cared for before being released into the wild again.

Scientists may also transport pandas that have been isolated in small areas to larger bamboo forests where there is more chance of survival. One serious problem is that bamboo plants in a particular area die off about every 50 years. In the past when that happened, pandas would be able to move to another area, where bamboo was flourishing. Now that their habitat is so restricted, there is less chance of their doing this successfully without human help.

The Chinese government has set aside special reserves where the panda is protected. But if the population in any area drops below about 40 or 50 animals, they are in danger of dying out.

The Chinese have had some success in breeding pandas in captivity. They hope to introduce zoo-bred pandas into the wild.

▽ A mother washes her baby, born in a Chinese zoo. The Chinese have been breeding pandas in captivity for many years, but until recently the survival rate was less than four out of ten. Better methods of looking after baby pandas have improved their chances of survival.

The lesser panda

The lesser panda is found in a large area of western Asia, from Nepal to southwestern China. It is also called the red, or common, panda.

Like the giant panda, it lives in high mountain forests and enjoys bamboo. But it eats a wide variety of food, including leaves, buds, roots, fruit, insects, eggs and even small birds.

△ The lesser panda is a beautiful animal, with thick, soft fur, which is a shiny red, or chestnut, on its back. Its face is mainly white. Its paws are turned in slightly, like the giant panda's, so it has an awkward, waddling walk.

◁ The lesser panda spends most of its time in the treetops. It is a nocturnal animal, sleeping during the day. The female usually has two cubs in the spring.

When attacked by other animals, the lesser panda can defend itself with long, sharp claws.

The story of pandas

△ French missionary Père David, the first westerner to see a giant panda.

The "black and white bear"

Giant pandas were unknown outside China before 1869. The first westerner to see and describe the animal was Père Armand David, a French missionary. He believed he had discovered a new black and white bear. But scientists thought it was more closely related to the red panda, and decided to call it the giant panda. Experts still cannot agree whether it is closer to the bear family or to the raccoons. The Chinese have long called it "bei-shung," meaning "white bear."

The giant panda comes west

It was many years before people in the west saw a live panda, although skins and dead specimens were acquired for museums in Europe and the United States. On a scientific expedition to Asia in 1928, two sons of former US president Theodore Roosevelt shot a giant panda. Other western hunters and explorers tried and failed to bring one back alive.

At last, in 1936, Ruth Harkness, a woman with no experience of animals or exploration, brought a baby panda back from China to the United States. With the help of an adventurous 20-year-old American, Quentin Young, she found the cub in the wild, kept it alive, and took it home. It was a remarkable achievement.

△ One of the first panda pelts to leave China, sent home by Père David.

△ The Roosevelt brothers, Theodore Jr. (left) and Kermit, the first western hunters to shoot a panda.

The popular panda

Zoos in some other countries acquired pandas, and they became star attractions. In 1958, the World Wildlife Fund, an international organization concerned with saving species from extinction, adopted the giant panda as its symbol.

Protecting the panda

The people of China are very proud of their famous animal. But, despite strenuous efforts by the Chinese government, the number of pandas has been declining steadily. Early in 1987, the World Wildlife Fund declared a "panda emergency." They launched a campaign to help China save the animals remaining. New measures were taken to protect their habitat and prevent small

groups from becoming isolated. Scientists stepped up their research into methods of breeding pandas in captivity.

Later in the year, the Chinese took the drastic step of introducing the death penalty for poachers who kill pandas and for anyone caught smuggling their pelts, which can be sold for several thousand dollars each.

△ Ruth Harkness, a New York clothes designer, caused a sensation when she arrived home from China in 1936 with a live giant panda cub.

29

Facts and records

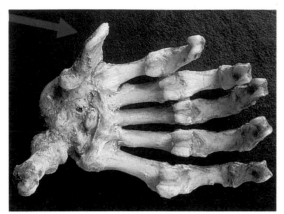

△ Skeleton of a panda forepaw, with sixth digit shown.

The sixth digit

On its forepaw, the giant panda has a sixth digit. This little bone, called the radial sesamoid, is covered with flesh to form a kind of thumb. It enables the panda to pick up and grasp bamboo. Such a skill is unequaled in the animal world except by the apes and monkeys.

△ Chinese writing for bei-shung, "white bear."

Most valuable exhibit

Few giant pandas have left China in recent years. Ling Ling and Yong Yong, on loan from China, were shown to large crowds at several US zoos in 1987.

△ Using the sixth digit.

△ Even in Chinese zoos, crowds flock to see a young giant panda.

Glossary

Bei-shung
The traditional Chinese name for the giant panda. It means white bear.

Breeding
The mating of animals to produce babies. Breeding giant pandas in captivity is extremely difficult. There are only a few days a year on which the female can mate successfully, and the male may not always be interested. In addition, when cubs are born, the survival rate is not high compared with other animals.

Digit
A finger or toe.

Extinction
The dying out of a species. The numbers of giant pandas are decreasing every year and they are in danger of becoming extinct. It was estimated in early 1987 that only 700 giant pandas were left in the wild, a decrease of 200 over 10 years.

Habitat
The place where a particular animal lives. The natural habitat of the giant panda is high up in the bamboo forests of central China. The panda is a very fussy animal and forages only in the shelter of tall trees that shade more than two-thirds of the ground. So if trees are cut down, even if there is a plentiful supply of bamboo, the pandas will look for new habitats.

Nocturnal
Active at night, and sleeping during the day.

Raccoon
A furry North American animal with a big, bushy tail, thought to be related to the pandas. Raccoons and lesser pandas are about the same size and have certain features in common.

Radial sesamoid
The little flesh-covered bone on a panda's forepaw, which enables it to grip such things as bamboo shoots. It is like a thumb.

Reserve
A special area set aside where animals and vegetation are protected.

Index